A MOUTH FULL *of* LUST

Sasha Nudél

www.sashanudel.com

ISBN: 9780578518633

Cover by Pride Nyasha

Illustrations and design by Victoria Shishkina

Editing by Lisa Cappiello

To love personified, my daughter Sienna.

Always be wildly curious.

Romanticize the ordinary.

Day-dream.

Feel.

Be kind.

I hope you enjoy the flip animation of
my heart's metamorphosis.

C O N T E N T S

LOVE RAW

Raw

Give me raw feelings.
Show me your flaws.
Tell me what moves you
and at your soul gnaws.

Perverted reflections,
all secrets you buried.
Your shameful reactions,
all loss your heart carried.

Your small talk is skin-deep.
Does not interest me.
If you're after my heart,
let me into your reverie.

Fetishes? Fantasies?
You're always unerring.
Get rid of all masks!
Perfection is boring.

I'll see your scars and raise you mistakes.
Just tell me all about your life's outtakes.
A messy mind is not a curse.
After all, my demons play so well with yours.

Gone are the days when I would protect my feelings by acting like I didn't have any.

I'm feeling and emoting now.

FaceTime

Real smiles crinkle the eyes.
Sidelong glances, breaths, and sighs.
Feeling robbed of that when I text to speak.
Face-to-face conversations is what I crave and seek.
Are you nervous? Are you gleaming?
How will I know you're happy to see me?
Gestures, movements, and expressions.
Your body language can answer all of my questions.
Would hate to miss out
on your Cheshire Cat mischievous grin,
when you're lazily hiding behind the computer screen.
Love watching you squirm and fidget
and hear your words get slurred.
Pretty sure I just learned that you blush when you flirt.
I'm such a glutton for endorphins and physical reactions.
Not at all am I into all the computerized interactions.
Broken telephone garbling is simply a shame.
"More social, less media" will be my game.

There's this one thing
to be made clear:
to find your passion
you must follow your fear.

Insatiable Thirst

The mere juxtaposition
of life and death
is so powerful,
it renders me incapable of anything
except trying to quench
the insatiable thirst that
being alive
has unearthed inside me.

Your heart will deflate a little with every passing
"what could've been" thought.

Keep it pumping.

Leap

No more "what-ifs,"
"one-days,"
and maybes."
You're in too deep.
You're not a cat,
you only have one life,
so take that leap.

You owe nothing to anyone and everything to time.

French Kiss

In my amorous
pursuit of happiness
I lock lips with life,
its good,
its bad,
its messiness.
Too much passion in me
for a friend zone.
I'm French kissing it.
Yes, tongue and all.

It takes so much effort to not be your authentic self.

Why even bother.

My heart is shedding tears for this Emoji culture.
You think being brave behind the telephone screen
makes you a fearless vulture.
Yet your boss' constructive criticism
for your self-proclaimed creative soul
is apparently too much structure.
Truths offend you and validation from strangers
is holding you hostage.
You live for groundless gossip with fake friends,
even though your social media addiction
has only made you more isolated.
Just acknowledge it!
But what do I know.
Maybe ignorance indeed is bliss.
Please, prove me wrong! Out-wit me!
I yearn for more knowledge.

Thou shalt start practicing what thou preach on social media.

Imagine

Mired by drudgery
off and even on social media
we all wish for an IV drip
of vitamin inspiration.
When instead,
we should simply
start using our imagination.

Soul for sale by owner. Only $inspiration.

Life After Death

There is still life after death for you
if you've ever inspired a poet.
Engraved in their verses.
Celebrated between the lines.
Praised in their musings.
Immortalized in their rhymes.

What's more addicting than feeling loved?
Feeling inspired.

Quiescent Heart

Arouse me from the lethargy
of my set ways
by challenging my beliefs.
Prick me into consciousness
with a sharp and witty point.
Provoke a feeling
inside my quiescent heart
and I promise
to make room for you in it.

Protect the jewel beating inside of your treasure chest.

Substance

Be picky about the human substance that
you introduce into your mind and body,
as it can be a vitamin,
a pain reliever,
or poison.

Sometimes,
waiting patiently
is a way of being proactive.

Borrowed Time

Exchanging big words frivolously
knowing we're on borrowed time.
Seriously!
If you're still caging your love rigidly,
mind bending its definition, possibly?
How can you not fall for people constantly?
And if you do,
let them know immediately,
before death hits-and-runs drunkenly.

Bucket List

Patience would be a virtue
if time didn't exist.
It sure isn't,
when you only have one lifetime
and a never-ending bucket list.

Time-lapse

The world is
crashing and burning,
self-destructing,
collapsing.
We're locking our eyes
in slow motion
while all that's around us
is time-lapsing.

What a dream it would be
to make it in life
as someone whose words others use
as their "words to live by."

Words

The omnipotent power of words.
Even at times when they're empty,
they're still sharp as swords.
They can break you, soothe you, and move you.
Fix you, turn you on, and confuse you.
Discourage, inspire, kill you, and heal.
But silence can be deadlier,
so just say how you feel!

Without books we are just empty shelves.

Intellectual Arousal

Intellectual arousal is a thing, you know.
Just watch me fidget
in the company of open-minded beings.
Unprejudiced, receptive,
willing to consider new ideas.
To quench experimental thirst
upon each other
inspiration generously we bestow.

Be with someone who stifles your insecurities
and not your self-expression.

Naked

If you aim to inspire,
get soulfully naked and mindfully raw.
Most will appreciate and admire.
Funny how others will leer, stalk,
and then pretend to ignore.

Know that by con·forming
you are con·ning yourself into living
as a bogus form of your true self.

Kinky

Life is kinky.
It bends you to its will,
rips you open,
caresses and feather-strokes you and then,
when you least expect it,
whips you.
It stings for some time, but then
pain starts to work into discomfort
and the discomfort into pleasure.
And then suddenly,
you're alive with more desire and more purpose.
Life is kinky.

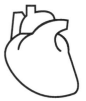

Unshackle

Rip off your insecurities.
Unshackle from society's confines.
Quit self-imposing limits.
Stop living your life on the sidelines.

Imagination

My imagination will be my demise,
but acting on it is worth the trouble,
worth the memories I make
before forevermore I close my eyes.

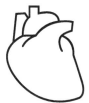

I hope you are so hyperaware of your mortality that you feel liberated to make every fleeting moment of your existence a memorable one.

LOVE LOST

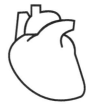

The Game

Both stared.
Both cursed.
Both cried.
Phones tossed.

He'd wait.
She'd hope.
He'd pray.
She'd mope.

Again she'd check.
He'd log back in.
With all this tech
and still no ring.

"I can't text first."
"One day I'll wait."
"He'll still be there."
"It won't be late."

Through fingers slipped
their time and flame.
With all this pride
both failed the 'game.'

Silence so ear-piercing, it's more telling than any of the spoken words.

To Whom It May Concern,

I can't stop the waterfalls.
I try not to be around people close to me now.
It's easier than having to explain my swollen eyes.
A passing thought about him triggers the tears and,
dear Google, clenching teeth, counting my breaths,
digging my nails into the palms of my hands does
not stand a chance when you're up against my
memories with him.

I'll take a memory-zapping device over a flying car
any day.

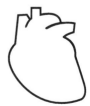

Maybe...

I should have locked my heart on you before you ever had a chance to commit homicide in its chambers. Maybe I'd still be alive.

Feigned Love

Hijacked my senses.
Stripped me of my skin.
Manhandled my rib cage.
Exposed the life-pumping sucker
just to rip it out of my chest with your filthy hands.
Patting yourself on the back now?
The irony is you think you won,
but all you have is
my deceased from your feigned love heart
and that shit is contagious, so disinfect.

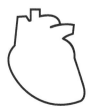

Two cynics don't cancel each other out.
So for the time being, let's pretend
we're both honest and hopelessly romantic.

Sixth Sense

I no longer have the taste of your laughter
in my mouth.
My eyes don't water when I picture you.
The thought of you no longer makes the hair
on the small of my back stand up.
Your scent has finally left all the layers of my skin.
I can no longer hear the echo of your sweet-nothings
I oh-so-foolishly believed. I've recovered.
But I now know that only someone with a sixth sense
could wreak havoc on all five of mine.

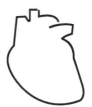

Your love is never wasted for you have once felt
inspired by that person.

Mosaic

Patching up my broken heart with words,
gluing the pieces back together with metaphors,
resurfacing with punctuation,
redecorating with rhymes,
beautifying my new mosaic art piece
in true artist's fashion.

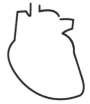

Bright Yellow

Somewhere between bright and dull
the sun and the earth
content yet restless and insatiable
my feet covered in dirt
yet hopelessly searching for that bright yellow
to leave me blind in love again.

LOVE HER

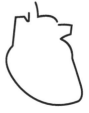

Poetry

Some times, I am structure, rhyme and reason.
Other times, I am free verse, confusion, and chaos.
I am poetry.

He who bothers to explore the bottomless ocean that is my mind is the one who gets to keep the sunken treasure.

Awakened Woman

You're so confused but still entrapped.
Keep peeping, waiting, stalking.
She piques your interest with her unapologetic self
and on your toes around her you're always walking.

So comfortable with all her passions, truths and flaws.
Enigma wrapped in barbwire.
She penetrates your mind
then leaves you sleepless and aroused.
She sets your soul on fire.

And if you're lucky to attract the eye
of this awakened woman,
she'll gift you magic, mystery, and self-realization.
She'll kiss, caress, and love you back to life.
You'll reap rewards beyond your mind's imagination.

If you are made to feel easily disposable,
make sure you're not recyclable.

Caution

You chose to trespass my soul.
I'm warning you: proceed with caution.
Over your mind you will no longer have control
for you have stirred a cauldron of intense emotion.

Once she dampens your edges with her tongue
and stamps you with her kiss, you're a sealed deal.

Untamable Fire

Unbothered, flat-affect, indifferent, cold.
Their unoriginal names for me are now getting old.
Untamable fire is what I'm inside.
A head full of thoughts: weird, blasphemous, wild.
If I look right through you smirking and grinning,
it's nothing personal. I am probably daydreaming.
Brave of you this conundrum that's me to try to define.
You still want a piece of me?
Then leave your comfort zone and fearlessly step into mine.

Too much ego will turn this lover into a leaver.

Lose Your Mind

Don't try to define me, just kiss me!
From my lips, to my neck
and all the way down my spine.
This is my warning.
You'll lose your mind
trying to understand mine.

Love her into eternity.
Kiss her into forever.
Touch her into oblivion.

Amusement Park

Being with her is like going to an amusement park.
She features various attractions,
such as emotional rollercoaster rides,
slippery water slopes, as well as entertaining mind games.
She induces panic and anxiety, hunger and satiation,
an adrenaline rush and crashing fatigue.
You leave exhausted but oh so high.

I am determined to make you fall in love with
poetry.

Ponytail

I can wear my hair down,
unoriginal, princess-like,
tamed and well kept.
But I'd rather move mountains
with my ponytail playful,
tenacious, wavy, and windswept.

I would need to see a rendering of your intentions
before I invest in your intellectual property.

Favorite Things

Breathtaking sunsets and freshly baked tarts,
unbroken promises, with new love smitten hearts,
views from a skyscraper, it's like I have wings.
These are a few of my favorite things.

Witty comebacks and respecting my time,
big juicy peaches and finding a rhyme,
music that moves you, when your crush sees you and winks.
These are a few of my favorite things.

Uninhibited chats, truths, dares, and merlot,
risk-worthy moments that make you utter "uh-oh,"
cool summer breeze caressing my heartstrings.
These are a few of my favorite things.

Soothing sound of waves, dancing, and skydiving,
late night adventures, being topless while driving,
my reminder to live when a pendulum swings.
These are a few of my favorite things.

Virtues

Kind-heartedness.
Open-mindedness.
Self-deprecation.
And chocolate with no hyphenation.

Masochist

Beware of a poetess
for she is not scared of a broken heart.
She's a masochist
who will simply turn you into a leading character
in her written art.

Watch your words with me.
I'll romanticize the poetry
out of every sentence.

Overrated

Stimulant personified
with her legs around your waist,
instant mood picker-upper
of mouthwatering taste.
She erects your alertness
and with your senses exacerbated,
she even makes coffee
sound overrated.

Worship

Worship her mouth
when "I love you" is said.
Honor the space between her legs
if you want them to spread.

Addictive

She's consciousness-altering,
euphoria-inducing,
pleasure-producing,
ecstasy-elevating,
bliss-creating,
dopamine-generating,
withdrawals-triggering
kind of dope.
For more of that addiction he couldn't help but hope.

Full

A platter of humor, wits, and manhood
to whet her appetite,
and finger-feeding her with that
until she's fully satisfied.

Color Palette

Mesmerized by the sky
reinventing itself daily:
from the innocent bright blue,
to filthy gray,
to cold charcoal,
to the morning's bright fairy-floss pink
with yellow undertones of melancholy.
From gloom to light, what a talent!
Mesmerized by life's color palette.

This Over That

You fascinate me
You're not like everyone else
You're so funny

_____

You're pretty
You're sexy
You have a great body

Feral

Trying to tame a lion after its escape from captivity
is less dangerous than trying to tame the feral butterflies
inside her chest.

Forbidden Fruit

I grew a forbidden fruit inside me so juicy,
it would be a fruitless endeavor
to try to pry yourself free of it.

Trendy Heart

Sensuality is her most flattering outfit.
That bold mouth accented with sparkly words
that complement a smirk so coquettish,
some call it their fetish.
A provocative glance
matches the way she always so proudly stands.
Head-to-toe trending is how she's perceived.
Except for the heart.
That one she wears on his sleeve.

Connoisseur

There was something
'arm's length' about her.
Often aloof, self-sufficient, demure.
Her attention so many
have failed to allure.
But it's hard to resist
the ultimate touch connoisseur.

Guided Tour

Welcome to her mouth.
On your left, you can see sarcasm and innuendos.
Poetry on the right.
Witty comebacks and snide remarks can be found
on the tip of her tongue.
The back of her throat is a place of great depth
and a point of no return.

This guided tour has been brought to you
by her latest prey.

LOVE AWAKENED

madness /ˈmæd·nəs/

noun:

the state of being severely foolishly illogically passionate

synonym:

love

For someone who always chooses her words accurately,
I can't believe I so recklessly professed my love for you.

Butterflies

sparks-in-the-eyes-butterflies-in-my-tummy-so-giddy-
I-look-silly-I-like-you-so-much-I-want-to-punch-you-
scratch-you-and-kiss-you-I-miss-you-all-day-and-all-
night-you're-my-favorite-sight-you-make-me-want-to-
rhyme-all-the-time
kind of love.

Grow Old

Legs intertwined, you fell asleep on my arm
completely contracting the space between us.
I knew I was in trouble when I wished I could
watch your chiseled face grow old.

Tautology

Abusing my poetic right to use tautology
in order to define our blazing flame.
Chaotically disordered, ardent heat is my analogy
for all the passion you ignite in me
and only you can tame.

Sure,
trust, respect and orgasms are necessary,
but next to the way you make me laugh,
they're secondary.

Consumed

I wish to write about the sun, the moon,
and the star-lit sky,
but you keep stealing my poems.
With you hiding between my lines
I forget what it's like to feel
clear-headed.

Anxious, impatient, and with impish glee
he watched her move towards him
as if he was one number away from winning the lottery.

Freudian Slip

My subconscious screaming his name over me
with all the Freudian slips of my tongue.
Wish it'd at least wait until he wasn't around.
But, no. All my poise out the window
as my lips he is watching.
I misspeak "looking" as "licking"
and for "teaching" say "touching."

She committed premeditated love last night and was life-sentenced to him.

Faint-hearted

Thought I was graceful until I stumbled
when you brushed up against me
and tripped upon you pulling me in.
Thought I was graceful until
I fell right onto your lap...
and for you.
Was it our chemistry or the vertigo?
This love thing sure isn't for the faint-hearted.
Now I know.

This moment with you will be just another poem
one day.

Autopsy

Why is it so hard to evenly
distribute my emotions?
Instead, my heart is infamous
for constant cuts and bleedings.
One day, I know I will get drunk
on yet another love potion.
And then my autopsy report will say
'she overdosed on feelings.'

Him: I'd sell my soul to kiss you right now.
Her: What a coincidence. It's just the currency that I accept.

Greedy For You

Our indelible passion, adventure,
and witty exchange of rib-tickling puns.
I'm greedy for that and for you.
Is that considered a 'pro' or one of the 'cons'?
Don't answer.
I know I've frequented your night dreams.
And now, I'm after your day ones.

Tipsy

You inebriate me,
my head is spinning,
and at my hedonistic apex
the taste of you
I can't stop swilling.

Chest To Chest

We have been wearing the sun all day.
Salty water embracing our feet.
Coral reefs keeping our fears at bay.
My breasts in need of your touch
are now enveloped in heat.

Twilight between my legs as we walk hand in hand.
Better yet, with your hand under my dress.
As the moon replaces the sun,
you and I chest to chest on the sand.

By the power vested in me by the law of serendipity,
I now pronounce you two body-, mind-, and soul-mates.

You may now stimulate each other.

Hijacked

It started with her soul, her mind, and heart intact.
Then they exchanged one smile, two jokes,
and eye contact.
All of her thoughts and daydreams he hijacked.
She lost her heart to him on impact.

When your battle of wits turns into a verbal intercourse
turns into soulful lovemaking.
That's the kind of relationship progression I'm into.

Incoherent

Losing control of my faculties
as your lips swallow my laugh,
your kisses muffle my moans,
and an unintelligible 'I love you'
escapes my mouth through
all the incoherent thoughts.
Is that what being
drunk in love feels like?

The strength of your arms around my waist
is directly proportional to the weakness in my
knees.

Unsteady

A failed attempt at trying to breathe
some steadiness into myself
after he upsets my balance
with just a couple of fingers
has me clawing his neck
to prevent my collapse
as I'm dizzily groping for air
hoping this moment lingers.

It was love at the first sight of his massive vocabulary.

Equation

Add your kisses and warm glances.
Subtract distance. Multiply your caresses.
Divide time apart and let's see where it gets us.
You plus me equals infinity. Love endlessly.
Bond so palpable, real life fantasy.
Math is too logical for our connection.
Beyond any reason is our attraction.
Our formula is made of irrational numbers.
Result of our addition:
you make my heart bang the loudest.

Silly of me to count on 26 letters to convey my feelings for you. Let me make a much stronger statement with all of my 206 bones.

Scientifically

"You have a premature ventricular contraction also
known as an extra heartbeat," the doctor announced.
"Sounds poetic," I whispered leaving him looking
perplexed. Even my cardiogram is overwhelmed with
the love I have for you. Now I understand why when
I rested on top of you postcoitally chest to chest,
together our heartbeats would sound like jazz.
Turns out I don't only love you poetically.
I also love you scientifically.

Do not promise me eternity as it is fundamentally unattainable. I can be easily pleased with your "now."

Cooing

I might seem calm and collected,
but as you're mouthing words at me
I'm trying to stomach the butterflies
and not let my chest show the somersaults
my heart is doing.
How loudly is my soul cooing?

He's so perfect, I'm at a loss for hashtags.

Dear Heart

Dear heart,
You owe me an apology!
For my irrational thoughts and smitten eyes.
All these feelings sure did catch me by surprise.

Dear heart, man up!
Raise the guard! Don't disappoint!
I'm simply saving you from breaking.
Exclamation point.

Feeling

That feeling...
What is it?
I can't put my finger on it.
So you do.
And not only one but two.

That feeling...
What is it?
You can't wrap your head around it.
So I do.
Why do you think that feeling just grew?

Rubik's Cube

Dissecting every word
and every move they're scrutinizing.
She's overthinking,
all of their texts he's overanalyzing.
Groping for words in order to
define this inexplicable sensation.
But it's as easy as solving one of Rubik's Cube's
quintillion configurations.
These feelings are so different
from anything they've felt before.
And as they stare, inside their heads both ask:
"How can I love you so?"

Mad Love

No use in finding the words
to define 'love,'
for when you're actually in it,
words don't really matter.
It's through the desperate
and irrational acts that love is felt
like those of the Mad Hatter.

Lover

Towering over me, my eye you caught.
Instantly drawn to you no matter how hard I fought.
Batting my lashes, timidly biting my lip.
Around my soul you're tightening your hand's grip.

With all your appeal and enticing bravado
you are my mind's and senses' aficionado.
You always match my effort and keep me on my toes.
Stronger my love for you with each day grows.

You stimulate my mind when needed
seducing me with tantalizing conversations,
yet gift me solitude to heal my erstwhile lacerations.
The sight of you in any weather,
any day is one I dearly behold.
I'm interested to see how our romance will unfold.

Your views incessantly set off a visceral reaction.
Forever you'll remain the subject
of my most intense affection.
It's funny how he thinks he has inspired my poetic spew.
When in reality, New York, my lover,
this poem's all about you.

"I'll take nothing less than all of you in exchange for more than your forever," he negotiated richly.

Spread-eagle

Love so uplifting
every time with him
she's sky soaring
in her head.
And when it's time to go,
she leaves her soul
spread-eagle
on his bed.

I have a soft spot for him and he has a hard one for me. That's our version of power exchange.

Time With You

Why are the best moments with you fleeting?
I'll stop tracking time!
Tossing all the clocks!
No longer needing them!

Why is time apart dragging?
No longer asking questions!
We can withstand the test of time,
so let's just keep laughing.

Them: How well do you know her?
Him: I can draw a map of her birthmarks with my eyes closed.

Touch

Some type of magic,
some kind of magnet,
some sort of alchemy
that made words useless
and touch -
the only means of communication.

His hand sought an opening in my blouse and I didn't have the heart to protest.

Throbbing

Judging by the shimmering lights
in my ocular periphery and
the pheromones my body emanates
when you intrude my aura,
I'm experiencing a throbbing euphoria.

Interactions filled with so many inside jokes and suggestive references, we sound like foreigners in our own city.

Favorite Place

How can I feel both protected
and most vulnerable in your embrace?
My safe haven and my battlefield
in that space.
Between your ear and your shoulder,
where I bury my face
is my favorite place.

Sonnet

Not even Shakespearean adjectives
to describe what love is
could compare to how she felt
when he simply called her his.

Battlefield

The brain and the heart went to war.
The first was a prude,
the insatiable second was constantly lusting for more.

The brain and the heart went to war.
The first got out safe and content.
The latter left shattered and bedabbled with gore.

I envy the air for the way it embraces you in all your entirety and the earth for caressing your feet as gravity pulls you toward me.

Palpable

Connection so palpable,
they'd lose their peripheral vision
in a crowded room.
Just two sets of eyes,
two racing hearts
making each other swoon.

Letters and sounds became obsolete and only physical contact could put their all-consuming passion into words.

Illogical

They fell for one another
against all logic
but with such conviction that
even the odds
gave way to their story.

Ours

Ours is the kind of love that
gives meaning to poetry,
harmonizes music,
and validates art.

Old

You obviously love my wild.
You definitely love me bold.
But will I still be on your mind
with body timid, frail, and old?

Too Late

Feelings professed on a rolled-up scrap of paper
inside an empty bottle set adrift on the ocean
were read by lovers
one lifetime too late.

Go text her now.

Shooting Star

Two mortals in love staring
at the vast expanse of stars
foreshadowing perfect weather
silently wish upon a shooting one
for a forever together.

Surrender

Running away from feelings?
Scared of this love much?
Don't be. Eventually,
even the wildest animal
surrenders to a gentle touch.

Modern Art

Every love story is different.
Ours too should be considered a form of art.
You fell for me while I was stroking your ego
then wrapped my legs around your head
and ate your way to my heart.

Please, please me.

MAKE LOVE

Wordsmith

My beloved wordsmith,
open up my pages,
place your finger on your favorite line.
Enunciate as you read it.
Add your name to my book's spine.

No time for circumlocution,
you need to fill in my blanks.
Answer all of my questions
with your hardcover between my legs.

Let's co-write our last chapter.
This love story is too grand.
Lust, passion, infatuation,
and a plot twist is that
there's no period at the end...

Foreplay

Foreplay does not always mean skin-to-skin.
Sometimes,
it's just inside jokes and eye contact
undressing each other from within.

Mother Tongue

You speak so eloquently to my body.
Touch must be your mother tongue.
You turn carnal sex into a night of poetry.
You whisper love haikus in my ear.
You transcribe verses on my neck with your tongue.
You read couplets to me with your fingertips.
You write sonnets on me with your lips.
You just finished a novel inside me
and it was the finest piece of literature I have ever read.
And that autograph on my heart
is just something to remember you by.

We are serenity lost and found inside the rippled bed sheets.

Wildfire

A wildfire inside me
set off by a spark
produced by a lightning strike
lit up by a kiss
caused by a mere touch
aroused by a lingering stare.

A wildfire inside me
doused in a shower booth
the moment our bodies we bare.

Remedy

Tormented.
Fix this!
My animalistic need.
Frantic, ardent, urgent sex.
Remedied.

Freeway

We're creating hazardous road conditions
as you track my curbs
disregarding the speed limit.
I'm manually operating your stick shift.
We're risking it all. So be it!
Fingers and mouths causing distractions.
Physical reactions of friction and traction.
No stop signs or red lights.
It's a freeway, technically.
I intend on crossing the finish line epically.

Impatient

Part my lips with yours.
Don't hesitate.
Trace, lick, and nibble.
For what I crave don't make me wait.

Tick Tock

First bellow ticks,
the second one tocks.
Pendulum swings.
Their time together it clocks.
Heart to heart clings
with each new deep thrust.
Pendulum swings.
They're cuckoo in lust.

Time-proof

Let's stay in our shatterproof bubble
with soundproof walls,
moisture-proof sheets
and make some time-proof memories.

Constellation

Out comes a constellation of memories
as this celestial body descends right onto mine.
The rapid rise of my chest,
the swell of my breasts
and we're levitated above cloud nine.

Supernova bursts into view
on the screen of a space radar.
And although we are to blame,
"Stay inside me,"
I wish on a falling star.

Big Bang

I am no cosmologist,
but I am certain
I just experienced an
explosion inside my universe
of the Big Bang caliber.

Explosion

With a bang of our clashing bones
and a crackle of bursting hearts,
with the moans of our yearning mouths
and the neediness of our arms,
with a swoosh of our rushing blood
and the slapping of bare skin,
from our lustful "oohs" and "ahhs"
to a blaring explosion within.

Equilibrium unsettled by your intensity.
Stumbling regret-free.

Connect2

Lips connect.
Fingers latch.
Eyes don't blink.
Staring match.

Trace my thigh.
Light caress.
Pants got tight.
Whispers "yes."

Arch my back.
Pull my hair.
Nails dig in.
I gasp for air.

Chest to chest.
No more space.
Deeper thrusts.
Slower pace.

Moving up.
Sliding down.
Forward-back.
I'm turned around.

Grab my waist.
My back you kiss.
You throb inside.
You pin my wrists.

Breaths rev up.
Moans loud and hard.
Clock-ticking stops.
We come apart.

Unmade beds,
because I'd rather we stayed attached at the hips
until we've completely run out of time.

No Touching

We made love. Clothes on, no touching.
Caressing each other's dreams,
tickling goals,
nibbling aspirations,
dirty-talking about our fears,
massaging inspirations,
fingering secrets,
licking minds' filthiest corners,
swallowing insecurities,
devouring heartbreaks,
toying with feelings,
laving emotional aches,
stroking egos,
satiating yearnings,
satisfying desire that's burning.
We made love. Clothes on, no touching.

You have the tastiest soul I have ever laid my mouth on.

.

Tap Tap

Fingertips typing words on her back
not brave enough to mouth to her face.
Commands. Controls. Shifts.
Enters her Space.

Taps into subconscious.
Tantric click Deletes all of the above.
Returns to her Home key.
Caps lock on Love.

"Come closer. Let me compromise the health of your heart by giving you a taste of my forte," she mouthed the words while kneeling in front of him.

Faith

It is certainly easier to believe in God
than to question his existence.
I have personally felt so much resistance.
Never imagined myself praying while kneeling,
until you gave me the most divine feeling.
Now, as I am on my knees in front of you,
batting my lashes,
butterflies teasing my core,
I can assure you, I am agnostic no more.

Vital Signs

Mouths dampened.
Flushed skin happened.
Heart rate accelerated.
Blood pressure elevated.
Breathing quickened.
The plot thickened.

Now, to stabilize your vital signs
there's only one thing left to do.
I simply need to be on top of you.

Maestro

Make music to my body with the same neediness
as when you pretend-play piano
upon hearing your favorite melody.
Touch harmony back into my skin
with your usual flair and aplomb.
Tap passionately into my energy, maestro,
leaving me spellbound by your body mechanics again.

Head Over Heels

Behind every girl who is head-over-heels in love
isn't a boy with a gimmicky jewelry prop.
There's a man who eagerly keeps her heels
over her head round-the-clock.
Mic drop.

Get A Room

The back-and-forth exchange
of "what I would do to you"
turned into a blur of kisses on the floor
leaving our bodies naked, hearts-consumed, lips-raw.
This does feel like something that might bloom,
but just for now,
it looks like the epitome of "get a room!"

Encore

Bravo! Encore!
As you can see my praise for you is gushing.
During tonight's performance,
even the fly up on that wall was blushing.

Braille

Pinned against the wall.
Smiling against your lips.
Your chest against my breasts.
The squirming of our hips.

Braille against my flesh.
Nail marks against your skin.
Throbbing against my core.
Slowly exploding within.

Shameless

Spooning lazily
while your hands wander eagerly
down my arched back teasingly
with my breasts engorged forwardly
all the feelings
            gushing
                    out of me
                            shamelessly.

Outdone

Well, that escalated quickly.
Our conversation.
From hobbies and passions to sharing our demons.
So refreshing!
Oops!
My adductors are tensing up in anticipation.
Being patient is causing frustration.
We're engaged in visceral penetration.
My soul straddling yours. Minds grinding.
Bringing us to the ultimate culmination.
All I did was ask for inspiration.
I'm impressed. Congratulations.
You have outdone my vivid imagination.

Oh My!

Binge-kissing.
Non-stop touching.
There's zero self-control.
Overindulging.
Oh my! Love seeing
how your pants are bulging.

Tongue Twister

Tempted to try to tame that throbbing taboo
inside your tight trousers as I tease
by tracing and tasting,
tormenting you with
the most tender tickle.
Touch traveling
to the epicenter of tension.
Hips thrusting towards me, mister.
I take it as you're enjoying my tongue twister?

Dead Arm

A round of applause for your dead arm
for cushioning my head
so I could share my dreams with you.
I'll gladly bring back the sensation in it.
And in other appendages too.

Flutter

He is tying her wrists and ankles
to his bed's corners,
but unlike others,
he is not going to cut her.
He's just turning that knot
in the pit of her stomach
into butterfly flutter.

Hologram

Oh baby, don't you fear
to go to sleep without tasting me?
My lover, can't you tell
my passion is why for me you fell.
Oh sweet face, don't you know
my elusiveness makes you crave me more?
Oh darling, can't you see
I'm just a hologram in your reverie.

Full Of Lust

Time together
slips through our fingers
as if it's sand.
Good thing wet sand
sticks better to your hand.
What's left to do but
clench our memories into a fist
of every gaze, kiss, moan, and thrust,
so we preserve the memory
of these two mouths full of lust.

Bare Soul

With your hands printed all over my flesh,
body silhouetted against the glass door,
I stand here with my soul
more exposed than my breasts,
burning, yearning, aching for more.

Boy+Girl

Boy meets girl.
He holds her in mind
since he first hears her speak
with that decadent grin.
In his head, a prey-catching plan
boy starts to scheme.

Girl makes boy lust after her.
A fantasy web boy starts to spin.
"Pardon me, you've excited my taste buds.
And now, I'm going in."

Coin Toss

Tonight, we're spinning bottles and flipping coins.
Heads, I taste your laughter in my mouth.
Tails, I make you feel a stirring in your loins.

Electric

An electric charge shocks my nerve endings as our
lips touch, flows through my veins into my head,
all of my previous kissing history combusts
leaving a blank slate for you to electrify.

Dreaming

Moans,
heavy breathing,
swearing, occasional pleading.
All the sounds emitted outdo any background music.
Dreaming with you wide awake and in lucid.

Pillow

I kept my pillow entertained last night
dreaming up a storm about you and I.
Heavy breaths, moans, and a lip bite.
Woke up with it pressed up against my inner thigh.

Good thing pillows can't talk.
Between my bedtime thoughts and my REM dreams
mine has a lot of compromising evidence on me.

Stop

What I mean when I breathlessly
beg you to "stop-stop-stop"
as you take me over the edge,
flip my insides
from horizontal to vertical
is that I want you to just
stop making everything
else in my life seem
so unremarkable.

Zero

Look. I really tried to keep
my impulses subdued,
but on a scale of null to self-control,
there's zero willpower
when it comes to you.

Fruition

This crowd's temporarily
taming my desire into submission.
Eyes locked on you,
I am now on a mission.
My desperation
spiraling to torturous depths,
just one kiss and my body's in chaos.
I am about to come to fruition.

Do Not Disturb

Putting on my best poker face in public
with this 'do not disturb' look on my face
as I get busy straddling you
in the privacy of my own mind.

Irony

The irony was in the reverence of his hand
wrapped around my throat
as he was professing his love
not knowing
he already had my heart in a chokehold.

That time you violated me across the room
with just one look. One arrogant, possessive,
high-handed look.
Do it again.

Oxymoron

The most possessively liberating,
firmly gentle handgrip
around the neck of someone
whose heart you own
houses the throat
that has numerously made you
grunt, groan, and moan.

Abracadabra

Sweet nothings in one ear,
dirty somethings in another.
And as I'm on his lap,
at me he looks.
I hear him whisper:
"Abracadabra, bra unhooks."

Cheers

Licked a dash of her soul off his moistened hand.
Downed her magic straight up and not on the rocks.
Chased her taste for a more intoxicating effect.
She's his shot of tequila that he licks, sips, and sucks.

Make her toes and the corners of her mouth curl.
It's that simple.

Shall We Dance

I sensed your presence
when I felt your breath on the small of my back.
I turned around and saw a famished bull
about to sink his teeth into my neck.
The way your grabbed my waist, yanked my arm,
ready to go in for a kiss.
"You're mine," you whispered
with your hand around my neck weakening my knees.
With your firm handgrip and perfect arm posture,
you create a stable embrace.
But in no time you're wild and aroused,
invading my personal space.
With prurient demeanor you dominate our tango.
With pleasure I submit.
You order me around the dance floor.
You make a perfect lead.
With loving fury you charge at me,
ripping my corset to expose my breasts.
So eager to devour what is the most prized
of all your previous conquests.
Slow-slow-quick-quick-slow is the rhythm of our tryst.
And as I'm savoring every moment,
our dance takes a pivotal twist.
My wrists pinned to the floor, eyes piercing me,
claiming my heart tête-à-tête.
You rip my skirt, spread my legs,
and shatter my earth at the click of the castanet.

On Hold

Black dress- his pick.
Bed hair- his fault.
She smiles- knees weak.
Time stops- world on hold.

Mine

We claimed each other differently.
He, by connecting my birthmarks with his tongue,
while I was covering ground with my nail marks.

You make my
mouth water,
head- high,
legs shake,
heart sigh.

Embrace

Wrinkled bed sheets,
rosy lips and white lace.
In my signature scent
I'm waiting for your embrace.

That decadent, scrumptious,
melt-in-your-mouth kiss
leaves you breathless, insatiable,
in pure finger-licking bliss.

Climax

Did I mention how much it turns me on
to watch you
in your element,
in all your glory?
Oh yes.
It did slip out of my mouth
while you were making sure
I reach the climax of this story.

ACKNOWLEDGMENTS

I am forever grateful for the support and encouragement I received from family and friends during the pursuit of this crazy dream of mine. Thank you to my husband, Igor, and my soul sisters, Alina and Natalie, for being my biggest cheerleaders. My deepest gratitude to my parents, Inna and Igor, whose love is with me always and forever. Many thanks to my editor, Lisa, for her continuous guidance. Thankful for those hiding between the lines of my poems. And to my lovely readers, thank you for reading and sharing my words.

ABOUT THE AUTHOR

Sasha Nudel is a Ukraine-born poet, speech-language pathologist, certified fitness trainer, and simply someone who is passionate about many things. Immigrating to the United States at the age of 16 inspired her to write about that experience. However, she put writing on hold to pursue her professional careers. It wasn't until she became a mother in 2015 that she felt awakened and inspired to put her thoughts, dreams, and fantasies into writing again. Sasha writes poems about love, relationships, sensuality, sexuality, and vulnerability with the hope of empowering women to feel confident and unapologetically true to themselves. She currently resides in Brooklyn, NY. You can follow Sasha's poetic journey on Instagram @a.mouthful.of.scribbles and www.sashanudel.com.

Made in the USA
Lexington, KY
28 October 2019